No One Is Coming

No One Is Coming

A Step-by-Step Guide to Healing, Rebuilding, and Thriving as a New Single Mom

Janaia Secrest-Holden

You Are the Hero of This Story

Table of Contents

Acknowledgments

First and foremost, I want to thank my son, Ayden. You've been my ride-or-die, my little partner in crime since the day you were born. Without you, this version of me wouldn't even exist. You've been my reason, my fuel, and my constant reminder of what I'm capable of. I love you more than words could ever say.

To my daughter, Ariah—you have pushed and pulled me in ways I didn't even know were possible. You are the light of our world. Through you, I see myself more clearly. You've given our little family this unexpected, beautiful bow that ties it all together. You were the missing piece we didn't even know we needed, and now we couldn't imagine life without you.

To my partner, Aaron—thank you for walking with me through this journey. For showing up first as a friend, and then becoming so much more. Your support, your presence, and your love has meant more than I can ever fully explain. You've held space for me, encouraged me, and been steady in the storm. I'm so grateful for you.

And lastly, to my parents—thank you for doing your absolute best, and I have to say, y'all did a pretty damn good job. Everything I am at my core is because of the two of you. Your love, your strength, your sacrifices, and your values shaped me into the woman I am today. I carry your legacy forward with pride.

I love you all deeply. This book wouldn't exist without you.

Introduction

I remember the day one of my really good friends came to my house. She and her partner had split up. They shared a son, and she was devastated. She didn't know what she was going to do. Watching her fall apart brought me right back to that moment when I was in her shoes, feeling exactly how she felt. I've been there. I understand the pain. And I told her the same harsh truth I'm going to share with you now: I wish I had something more positive or inspirational to say, but the truth is, it's going to suck. And it's going to suck really bad for a while. But it will get better.

No One Is Coming

The harsh reality is that no one is coming to save you. This new reality you've been forced into is what it is. And as much as it sucks—and again, it's going to suck for a while—it does get better. But how your story goes from here is completely up to you.

I understand exactly how you feel. I understand the overwhelming struggle of being left to pick up the pieces from a decision you didn't make. And even if you did make the decision to leave, you still have to mourn the loss of your relationship, the loss of the future you thought you had, the loss of the family you were building. I know what it's like to feel betrayed. To trust somebody with your heart and your future only for them to fumble you, to mistreat you. To give your love and care to someone who doesn't give it back. I know what it's like to be heartbroken, devastated. To ask yourself all the what-ifs and how-could-I's. To go back and forth in your mind about what you could have done better, what you should have recognized earlier.

And yes, there's always a part of accountability in any situation, but I want to make one thing clear: It's not your fault. With every trial, there's a possibility of a triumph. The most important thing to understand is that when you go through something like this, when you experience the kind of pain, struggle, and heartbreak you're going through right now, you only have to go through it once—if you learn from it. If you pull forth the lessons and rebuild a stronger, more confident, more resilient, and more secure version of yourself.

I know the feeling of starting over from scratch. I know what it feels like to give up your friends, your family, your career, to put your all into the family you thought you were building. I know what it's like to walk away—or be walked away from—with nothing and literally have to rebuild your life from nothing.

And although it may not feel like it right now, I can promise you, and this book promises, that you can rebuild your life. I've been where you are, and I've done it. I'm not special. So, if I can do it, I know that you can too. I've helped other women do it. And throughout history, women have been doing it. You are stronger than you know or feel right now.

This book is going to guide you through healing your heart, rebuilding your finances, and creating a future you're proud of. A life you love. Something beautiful.

The book is broken up into three major parts — three areas you need to work on to reach the light at the end of the tunnel. The first part focuses on Emotional Healing. Because right now, you can't build anything while you're still hurting and broken. You have to heal. You have to pick yourself up and work on mending your heart and building yourself from the inside out.

The second part focuses on Rebuilding Your Finances. Let's face it: money doesn't buy happiness, but it sure can alleviate a whole lot of stress when it's taken care of. Financial security is incredibly important, especially as a single mom.

The last part is about Reinventing Yourself. It's about getting clear on the woman you want to be, the mother you want to be, the future partner and wife you want to be. Because this isn't the end of your story. It's just a chapter. And as long as you're still breathing, you have the ability to grow, to evolve, and to become whoever it is you want to be.

I know your time is precious. As a single mom, you don't have time to waste on long, drawn-out books. So, this one is designed to be brief and to the point, giving you everything you need to heal, create security, and become the next best version of yourself. Brief and valuable. That's the goal.

I know everything hurts right now. I know you may find yourself crying in the shower or in the middle of the night. There will be highs and there will be lows. And I won't lie to you—it won't be easy. But you're not alone. You're capable of healing. You're capable of rebuilding. And you're capable of creating the life you want. The life you dream of. Not only are you capable, but you're deserving.

Others have been exactly where you are and have rebuilt themselves stronger. I've been where you are, and I've come out on the other side. I know what the journey looks like, but I also know the glory that you're going to walk into. The wholeness, the warmth, the love. It's great over here. You don't see it now, but you will. That, I promise.

Part 1

Emotional Healing & Rebuilding

Chapter 1

Accepting Your New Reality

They say there are five stages of grief after a loss. And yes, the loss of a relationship absolutely counts as a loss. You have to go through those stages of grief: denial, anger, bargaining, depression, and finally, acceptance. I remember going through all of these stages, and just when I thought I was done with one, I'd circle right back to it. It's a messy, unpredictable process. Maybe you can relate to that.

Accepting Your New Reality

When I first found out about my ex cheating, I was in denial. Everything I believed about him, every reason I thought I chose him, didn't match up with someone who would step out on our relationship. I felt completely blindsided. It felt impossible. And so, I stayed in denial for way too long.

Once the truth settled in, the anger hit me hard. And this is where the "bitter baby mama" phase rears its ugly head. We definitely don't want to get stuck here. Because even though it's justified and completely natural to be angry, staying in that place only hurts you. Not him. Not anyone else. Just you. Holding on to anger is like drinking poison and expecting someone else to die.

Now, I'm not saying you don't have a right to be angry. Hell, you probably have every right to be. And you should feel those emotions. You may even have to crash out a time or two. Scream. Cry. Vent to your friends. Journal. Go to therapy. Whatever it takes. Just don't stay there. Because nothing done out of anger is ever good.

Then comes the bargaining. And this is the part where we start picking ourselves apart. "Maybe if I lost a little weight." "Maybe if I cooked more." "Maybe if I had been more understanding, supportive, or less demanding." We go through every single detail of the relationship, convincing ourselves that if we had just been a little bit better, a little bit more, then things would've turned out differently. But that's a lie.

His choices were his own. Whether he cheated or left or simply stopped caring, that was his decision. Not yours. And trying to convince yourself that you could've changed the outcome by being someone you weren't only drags you further down.

Now, let's talk about the depression. And I'm not going to sugarcoat it. Depression is brutal. It's the stage that lingers over all the others, hovering over your grief like a dark cloud. It's heavy, it's consuming, and it feels never-ending. It steals your energy, your motivation, your joy. And just when you think you're moving on, that depression shows up again and reminds you just how shattered you are.

But then, there's acceptance. And this is where the real healing begins. Acceptance is when you stop looking in the rearview mirror and start looking ahead. It's when you recognize that it is what it is. It's not what you planned. It's not what you wanted. But it's real. And it's yours to rebuild.

Acceptance doesn't mean you're over it or that you've forgiven or forgotten. It just means you've come to terms with the fact that things didn't go the way you hoped. Acceptance lets you pull the lessons from the wreckage and start building something better. It's the place where you finally understand where you are so you can figure out where you want to go.

Acknowledge the Pain

One of the hardest things you'll ever do is acknowledge the crushing reality that your relationship is over. And as if finding out about the cheating or being abandoned wasn't bad enough, you now have to come to terms with what it all means. That future you thought you had. It's gone. That dream of raising your children together. Gone.

No, it will never feel fair. And sometimes you may want to go full-on Carrie Underwood or Jazmine Sullivan—keying cars and smashing windows. Trust me, I've thought about it all. And sometimes it was only the thought of jail time or the image of my son's innocent face that kept me from spazzing and completely fucking shit up.

But as much as it hurts, you have to face the pain. You have to feel it, process it, and go through it. That's the only way you'll ever be able to move on.

Grieving What Was Lost

We do a lot of things when we're in love. We make plans. We make sacrifices. We make decisions based on the belief that this person will be our forever. We move across the country. We give up promotions. We build entire futures around them. And then one day, it's gone.

You're not just grieving the person. You're grieving the life you built in your mind. The future you imagined. The idea of raising your kids together under the same roof. And that can feel like failure. Like you failed them. Like you failed yourself.

But here's the thing. Sometimes life doesn't go the way you planned. And that's okay. It's equally important for your children to see you pivot, to see you grow from adversity. Because that's real life. And you are stronger than you think.

The Power of Acceptance

Acceptance is the first step toward healing because it's where clarity begins. It's the acknowledgment of where you are. Because without knowing where you are, you can't begin to build a roadmap to where you want to be. Think of it like GPS. You can't get directions from Los Angeles to Miami unless you first enter your starting point.

Acceptance is that starting point. It's acknowledging what's gone, what's broken, and what's left to rebuild. It's giving yourself permission to feel every messy, ugly, painful emotion and then deciding to move forward anyway.

Practical Steps

I'm not just going to tell you to "feel the feels" and leave it at that. You need action steps. You need something real.

- Therapy: If you can, find a good therapist. Someone you vibe with. Someone you can trust. Many workplaces offer Employee Assistance Programs (EAP) that provide free therapy sessions. Use them. There's no shame in taking advantage of the resources available to you.

- Journaling: Write out your emotions. Every single one. The anger, the sadness, the grief. Pour it all onto the page. And if you need to write a long text to your ex, do it in your journal instead of sending it. You'll thank yourself later.

- Presence: Be present with your children. Those moments of joy, no matter how small, will remind you that happiness still exists. Even in the middle of the storm.

Here's the thing: you have to go through the pain to get through the pain. There's no shortcut. It's ugly. It's brutal. It will tear you down. But it will also build you back up if you let it. And you, my beautiful, resilient friend, are more than capable of doing it. Acceptance isn't the end of the healing journey; it's the beginning.

Now that you've acknowledged your pain and accepted your new reality, it's time to start mending what's been broken. Healing from heartbreak is a process. And that's where we're going next.

Chapter 2

Healing from Heartbreak

There's a quote by Steve Harvey that says, "You have survived 100% of your worst days." Let that sink in for a moment. Even though the heartbreak you're facing right now feels unbearable, you've survived every painful moment life has thrown at you before. And you'll survive this too.

This isn't the first time you've felt hurt, betrayed, or let down by someone. And I hate to be the bearer of bad news, but it probably won't be the last. The truth is, human beings are imperfect, and every single one of us is capable of making mistakes — including you. Because we are wired to love and to be loved, heartbreak from time to time is just part of the deal.

But here's the difference: Just like you've healed before, your broken heart will heal again. The only thing that can stop that healing from happening is you. Some people choose to stay broken, clinging to a victim mindset. As backward as it sounds, they get used to living in the pain. They become addicted to the sympathy and empathy from others when they tell their sad stories. But staying in that place of brokenness never allows you to truly heal. And you deserve so much better than that. You deserve joy, love, peace, and happiness.

Processing Betrayal and Loss

Everyone handles betrayal and loss differently. And while there's no "right" way to do it, there are definitely some ways that can keep you stuck. The truth is, if you end up on Snapped, it's safe to say you chose the wrong way.

No One Is Coming

It's easy to feel like life has been completely unfair to you. Like you did all the right things, gave all of yourself to this relationship, only for it to fall apart. You feel betrayed by the person you trusted most, the person you believed would love and protect you. Processing that betrayal is no simple task.

One of the best ways I've found to confront and process those feelings is through empathy. And I know that sounds insane. Being empathetic toward the person who hurt you feels impossible. But here's the thing: Their actions have nothing to do with you and everything to do with them. As they say, "hurt people hurt people." Their betrayal, their abandonment — all of it speaks to the battles they are having within themselves. Not you. It's not your fault. And honestly, it's their loss.

Rebuilding Self-Worth and Confidence

I remember reading something from Mel Robbins that hit me hard. She said, "You were not born to be a wife." That's powerful because so often, we tie our worth and identity to our relationship status. But here's the truth: Whether you are single, married, divorced, or somewhere in between, your worth remains the same.

Good relationships are beautiful, and wanting love and partnership is completely natural. But your value as a person exists independently of any relationship. Every amazing quality you possess still exists whether someone recognizes it or not.

Rebuilding your confidence and self-worth starts with remembering who you were before the heartbreak. Who were you before the pain? What made you laugh? What made you feel alive? Sometimes, we lose ourselves in relationships. We forget who we are outside of being a mother, a girlfriend, a wife. And this process is about reconnecting with her. Reconnecting with you.

Emotional Healing Tools

Your journal is your best friend right now. It's where you can spill every single messy, complicated, and painful thought without judgment. Writing it out allows you to get it out of your head, and sometimes, that's the only way to make sense of what you're feeling.

Here are some journal prompts to help you process and release the pain:

- How am I feeling right now? What triggered these emotions?

- If I move out of my heart and into my mind, what do I think about how I feel and why that trigger has affected me?

- What makes me feel so attached to this person? How can I fulfill myself without them?

- Who was I before this person? Who was I during this relationship? Who will I be after?

- Describe everything you are feeling right now and everything you want to let go of.

- List three reasons why your ex was not the right person for you.

- List ten reasons why getting back together would never work.

Affirmations for Emotional Healing and Self-Love

Now, I know affirmations might sound corny. But there's real science behind it. Your brain can't tell the difference between something you vividly imagine and something that's actually happening. The more you tell yourself something, the more you start to believe it and embody it. You can literally change your mindset and emotional state with consistent affirmations.

Here are some affirmations to help you heal:

- Each day I am becoming stronger and more resilient.

- I forgive myself and others, freeing myself from emotional burdens.

- I let go of past hurts and embrace a future filled with peace and joy.

- I am worthy of self-care, and I prioritize my emotional well-being.

- I am enough just as I am.

- I am deserving of all good things in life.

- I am proud of who I am becoming.

Healing is not a straight line. It's more like a rollercoaster. There will be high points where you feel like you're finally getting better. Then there will be low points where you feel like you're right back at square one. But the truth is, as long as you keep moving forward, you're still making progress.

Every time you journal, every time you speak affirmations over yourself, every time you choose not to let the pain consume you — you are healing. And one day, you'll look back and realize that the hurt isn't as sharp, the sadness isn't as heavy, and you've rebuilt yourself stronger than ever.

But healing your heart is only part of the process. Because if you have children with this person, there's a whole other layer of complexity that makes moving on even harder. Co-parenting with someone who broke you is one of the most challenging things you'll ever have to do. But it's not impossible.

Let's talk about how to do that.

Chapter 3

Co-Parenting with the Person Who Broke You

The person you have children with is one of the most important decisions you'll ever make. Some people argue that the person you marry is the most important decision, but I would challenge that. If you marry someone and get divorced with no children involved, you can walk away and never have to deal with them again. No harm, no foul.

But when you share children with someone, you're tied to them — almost forever. You'd like to think it's just for the first 18 years, but the reality is they'll be your children for the rest of your life. Every milestone — graduations, weddings, grandchildren — all of those moments will tie you and your ex together. Even if you're not directly dealing with them, you'll see parts of them in your kids because let's face it, your children are half of them, too. And yeah, that can be annoying. But it's the reality of the situation.

Navigating co-parenting while healing from the person who broke you is a whole new challenge. Because while you're trying to heal and move on, you still have to interact with them. You don't get the luxury of completely cutting them out of your life. But here's the good news: It's possible. And if it's been done before, then it's doable. Use me as a testament to that.

You can absolutely co-parent and even have a healthy co-parenting relationship with the person who hurt you. But it's going to take a few things to make this work as smoothly as possible, given the circumstances.

Setting Healthy Boundaries

One of the most important things you need to do, and do early, is set healthy boundaries. This is how you protect your peace while remaining cooperative for your child's sake. Because regardless of the bullshit between you and your ex, they're still your child's father. And more than likely, your child still loves them. They may have been a crappy partner, but if they're a good dad, your kid doesn't know the difference. And they shouldn't. It's not their job to worry about your broken relationship.

You're not their wife or girlfriend anymore. Some responsibilities are not yours to carry. And let's be real, some of those responsibilities you definitely don't need to be picking up ever again. Factory closed.

When you communicate with them, make it about the kids and only the kids. And I know that's easier said than done when you're still hurting, but it's necessary. If they text or call you and it's not about the kids, you have every right to ignore it or redirect the conversation back to what actually matters — your children. And girl, absolutely leave those nonsense text messages on read. Keep those read receipts on. He'll get the picture.

Detaching Emotionally

You may hate your ex, or maybe you're just hurt by them. You might be angry, sad, or just over the whole situation. Whatever you feel, it's important to learn to detach your emotions from the co-parenting situation. You have to build the muscle of focusing on your child's well-being over your past hurt.

If your ex is a good father, let him be a good father. It's not your job to nurture their relationship, but it's your job not to hinder it. When I say that, I mean if your ex is genuinely trying to be there for your child, let them. Don't let your own pain get in the way of something good for your kid.

And let me be clear, if he's not stepping up, that's a whole different story. You can't force him to be a good dad. You can only control what you do. But if he's genuinely making an effort, then that's something you have to respect.

Practicing Grace and Patience

Now, this one is going to require you to dig deep. You need to practice grace and patience for yourself, your children, and yes, even your ex. All of you are trying to navigate new territory. You're healing from a broken heart and establishing boundaries. Your child is learning how to adjust to having their parents in two separate households. And your ex? They're adjusting to this new dynamic, too.

That doesn't excuse their past actions. But it does mean that you're all learning, and there are going to be some growing pains. You're not responsible for their growth, but you are responsible for your own healing. Be gentle with yourself. And remember, this is a process.

Practical Steps

Here are some practical steps to help you navigate co-parenting while healing:

- Keep Communication Child-Focused: Don't get into emotional or accusatory conversations. If they text or call about something unrelated to the kids, ignore it or redirect the conversation.

- Create a Co-Parenting Plan: If you can, try to work with them to create a parenting plan that outlines responsibilities, schedules, and boundaries. And if you can't agree on one, consider going through the courts if necessary.

- Give Yourself Permission to Walk Away: If conversations are getting too heated, it's okay to take a break and come back to it later with a clearer mind. Cooler heads always prevail.

I'm not going to lie to you — co-parenting with someone who hurt you is hard. It took me a long time to get to a good place with my son's dad. It was rocky, emotional, and at times, I questioned whether we'd ever get to a point where we could actually co-parent without conflict. But over time, we figured it out.

No One Is Coming

We've been co-parenting for almost a decade now. We've both moved on, and we're even able to do things collectively as one big, blended family. It may sound impossible to you right now, but I promise it's possible.

But here's the thing: Co-parenting successfully requires a mindset shift. It requires you to take your power back. You have to decide that you're no longer going to let the past control your present. You're no longer going to let someone else's actions keep you stuck in bitterness and pain. And that's where we're going next.

Chapter 4

Shifting Your Mindset from Victim to Victor

There's this powerful book called Mindset by Carol Dweck, and it breaks down the difference between having a growth mindset and having a fixed one. The truth is, everything we do or don't do stems from how we think. If we constantly see ourselves as victims — always saying, "Why me?" or "Life isn't fair" or "Look at what I've been through" — we stay stuck. That lens becomes the filter through which we see everything, and until we change the way we think, we can't change our lives.

Our brain has something called the Reticular Activating System (RAS) — think of it like a personal assistant for your mind. It filters the millions of bits of information we take in every second and decides what to focus on based on what it thinks is important to us. If you're always focused on how hard life is, how unfair everything feels, or how you've been wronged, your RAS says, "Okay, she wants more of that," and filters your world accordingly. That's why when you're having a bad day, it seems like everything just keeps going wrong. But when you're having a good day, even when something frustrating happens — like getting stuck in traffic — it doesn't throw you off the same way.

It's not because your circumstances magically improved. It's because your mindset did.

Shifting your mindset doesn't mean pretending everything is okay when it's not. It means intentionally choosing to see the good, to search for the lesson, and to decide that you are not going to stay stuck. Yes, that relationship ended. Yes, the family you dreamed of fell apart. But that doesn't mean your story is over. It doesn't mean you won't have a new chapter filled with more love, more peace, and more joy than ever before.

And let me say this clearly: no one else can do this mindset shift for you. It's completely on you. It doesn't matter how much your friends encourage you, how many books you read, or how many quotes you post to your Instagram story. If you don't actually believe that you can shift from victim to victor, nothing will change.

Two people can go through the exact same situation and come out of it completely different. One becomes bitter. The other becomes better. What's the difference? Mindset.

You can't control what happens to you, but you can always control how you respond.

And let's be honest — you don't want to give that power away to anyone else. Your healing, your future, your joy… those things belong to you. And when you hand them over to someone else — especially someone who hurt you — you give them way too much control. You are the main character in your life. Everyone else is a supporting role, and your healing is your responsibility.

So, what does that look like in real time? It means being mindful of your thoughts. It means catching yourself in those negative spirals — those moments when you feel like everything is falling apart — and saying, "Hold up. This is a victim mindset. And I'm not a victim. I'm a victor. I'm still here. I'm still breathing. I'm still standing. So, I'm still growing."

It means saying to yourself: There's something in this pain for me. I just have to find it.

Training Your Brain for Victory

If you've ever watched a motivational video or heard a successful person talk about how they made it through something hard, they almost always mention visualization and affirmation. Why? Because it works.

Shifting Your Mindset from Victim to Victor

Your brain can't tell the difference between a real experience and one you've vividly imagined. That's why athletes visualize their performance before they ever step onto the field. Michael Phelps, one of the most decorated Olympians of all time, used visualization before every single race. He'd mentally walk through the perfect swim — and then he'd walk through everything that could go wrong and how he'd handle it. By the time he actually raced, he had already lived those moments in his mind.

So why not do the same with your healing?

Think of the next best version of yourself — not some fantasy version, but the real woman inside of you who's just waiting for her moment. What does she do when she wakes up in the morning? What does she wear? How does she talk? How does she respond when her ex tries to stir up drama? How does she handle stress, joy, dating, motherhood?

Visualize her every single day. Carve out 5–10 minutes a day — maybe in the morning or right before bed — and see her in your mind. Feel her energy. Feel the peace she walks in. And remind yourself: That's me. That version of me already exists. I'm just becoming her, one day at a time.

And then speak life over yourself — even when you don't feel like it. Especially when you don't feel like it.

Custom Affirmations for a Victor's Mindset

Here's how you create affirmations that work: identify how you feel right now, and then write the opposite of that feeling as a present-tense statement.

If you feel heartbroken, your affirmation might be:

I am healing with grace, strength, and peace.

If you feel anxious:

I am grounded, calm, and in control of my emotions.

If you feel weak:

I am powerful. I have everything I need to move forward.

Repeat these affirmations throughout the day. Write them on sticky notes. Record yourself saying them and play them back. Speak them every morning, at lunch, and before bed. Repetition rewires your mind.

Turning Pain into Power

As painful as all this is, I promise there's something good that will come from it. There is clarity in pain. There is direction in heartbreak. When I finally started dating again after my relationship ended, I had a blast. I really did. Not because every man I met was amazing (trust me, they weren't), but because I had a completely different mindset.

I knew what I didn't want. That clarity came from my pain. I didn't look at dating through the lens of "all men are trash." I looked at it as a sifting process. Every date showed me more of what I wanted and what I deserved.

So many of my single friends were miserable, frustrated, and discouraged. But I was having fun, learning, evolving. Why? Mindset. I wasn't chasing perfection. I wasn't expecting fairy tales. I was grounded in who I was and what I was looking for. That came from going through the fire and learning the lessons. My pain sharpened me.

And it will sharpen you too.

You'll be able to say, "Nope, that's a red flag," or "That's not for me," without guilt or second-guessing. You'll become a better decision-maker because clarity breeds confidence. And confidence gives you the power to walk away from anything or anyone that doesn't serve your future.

Practical Steps to Shift from Victim to Victor

Let's get into action.

- Create personalized affirmations: Start by identifying your current emotions and then write affirmations that affirm the opposite, more empowered state.

- Use them consistently: Say them out loud in the mirror, record them in your phone and listen to them, or write them in your journal. Make this part of your daily ritual.

- Practice visualization: If vision boards work for you, create one — but make it personal. Find images that truly reflect your desires, not generic magazine clippings. Put a picture of your happiest self on it. Visualize your dream life every day.

- Try scripting: If you're more of a writer than a visual person, write a "day in the life" journal entry as your next best self. Write in detail — where you go, what you wear, how you feel, what you do, who you love, and who loves you.

This is about embodying the energy of the woman you're becoming — not waiting for her to show up but deciding she's already here.

Reclaiming Responsibility for Your Life

The moment everything shifted for me was the moment I took back responsibility for my happiness. It was no longer about what my ex did or didn't do. It was about what I was going to do with what was left.

When we blame others, we give away our power. We make our healing someone else's job. And if they don't show up and handle it — which, let's be real, they rarely do — our world falls apart again.

Never forget you are your greatest project. The most important work you'll ever do is the work you do on yourself. And you do not want to leave your final grade in life in the hands of someone who failed you.

You are not a victim of your circumstances. You are the creator of your future. That version of you that you keep imagining. She exists. She's already real. You're just catching up to her.

I once saw a TikTok that said the reason we have certain dreams or desires is because a version of us already has them. That future already exists. And the only thing standing between you, and it is you. Your mindset. Your belief system. Your willingness to grow and shift and evolve.

Because what we think determines what we believe. What we believe shapes what we do. And what we do creates the life we live.

You already have everything you need.

Even if you don't feel confident yet — act like it. Because the truth is, the more you act like the woman you want to be, the faster you'll become her. And eventually, you'll look back and barely recognize the girl who once felt broken and lost. Because she stepped into her power.

And now? She's unstoppable.

You've started doing the internal work — you've been healing, shifting your mindset, and showing up for yourself in ways you probably didn't even think were possible a few months ago. And no, it's not a done deal

— it's still a process. There will still be days that test you, moments that bring up old feelings, and triggers that remind you of the past. But the fact that you're here, reading this, means you're in it. You're doing it.

This is the glow-up in motion. You've laid the foundation. Now it's time to channel that boss bitch energy into the next layer of your transformation: rebuilding your financial life. Because let me tell you — something shifts when your money starts looking right. Your confidence levels up. Your energy shifts. Your peace gets protected differently. When the financial stress starts to ease, you breathe deeper. You think clearer. You walk different.

Shifting your mindset was the beginning, but now we step into something just as powerful — building a life where you're not just emotionally whole, but financially strong too. A life where you don't just survive, you thrive.

Part 2

Financial Rebuilding & Empowerment

Chapter 5

Rebuilding from Nothing

Maybe this isn't your exact situation, but it was absolutely mine. When my relationship with my son's father ended, we were living in Hawaii, thousands of miles away from family and friends. So, when I left him, I didn't just leave the relationship — I left our home, our life, and the job I had. I packed up my 2-year-old, whatever I could fit in a suitcase, and moved across the Pacific Ocean back to my mother's house.

And let me tell you — I was grateful, but whew. Moving back in with my mom as an adult with a toddler? That will humble you quick. I love my mom, but there's a reason we all move out when we're grown. Still, her being able to take us in rent-free gave me a starting point. And that's all I needed. A starting point.

I had no job. No savings. No plan. Just me, my baby, and the reality that I had to rebuild from scratch.

So how do you do that? How do you rebuild financially when you're starting with literally nothing?

Know Your Starting Point

Before you can change your finances, you have to face them. You've got to know what you're working with. That means getting brutally honest. How much money are you bringing in? How much is going out? What's your actual cash flow — not what you think it is, but what it really is?

This isn't the time for ballpark guesses. Pull up your bank statements. Look at your last 3 months of transactions. Track every dollar. Food, gas, Target runs, Amazon orders, Apple Music, Netflix, Door Dash — all of it. You need to know where your money is going so you can tell it where to go going forward.

It might be uncomfortable. It might be ugly. But do it anyway. We're not in denial anymore — we're in rebuild mode.

Create a Budget That Works for You

I know, I know. The dreaded "B" word — budget. But hear me out. A budget isn't punishment. It's a plan. It's how you take control. It's how you tell your money what to do instead of wondering where it went.

One of the biggest challenges I had when I was rebuilding was realizing that most financial advice out there wasn't made with single moms in mind. Some of it didn't account for the fact that yes, I needed to cut back — but I also still wanted to make sure my son had a good childhood.

So, you need a budget that reflects your reality. One that's practical. One that includes necessities like rent, utilities, food, transportation, and yes — even some fun. You don't have to cut out everything. But you do have to be intentional.

Start with the basics:

- What's coming in?

- What has to go out?

- What can be cut or adjusted?

Netflix? Might have to go. Eating out? Probably need to dial that way back. Those little charges — coffee, fast food, subscriptions — they add up. Give every dollar a job. Every single one.

Build Your Emergency Fund (Even If It's Just $5 at a Time)

Now that you've got a budget, your next priority is building an emergency fund. Because life will life, sis. It's not if something unexpected happens — it's when.

I remember a season when I was getting flat tires like it was a full-time job. I swear my Hyundai had it out for me. But because I had started putting aside a little emergency fund, I didn't panic. I had a buffer. And that buffer gave me peace.

Start small if you have to. $5. $10. The key is consistency.

Try these:

- Use your bank's roundup feature (where your debit purchases round up to the nearest dollar and the difference goes into savings).

- Set up a direct deposit that automatically sends a small percentage (even 5-10%) of your paycheck to a high-yield online savings account. I personally use Ally, but there are several good ones out there.

- Keep your emergency fund separate from your regular bank, so you're not tempted to dip into it.

Out of sight, out of mind. But there when you need it.

Learn Basic Financial Literacy

You don't need to become a financial guru overnight, but you do need to understand the basics. Learn how money works. Get curious. Read books. Watch YouTube videos. Follow personal finance creators online who speak to your situation.

A great book to start with: I Will Teach You to Be Rich by Ramit Sethi. He doesn't shame you for wanting to enjoy life. He just teaches you how to plan for it. He even has a Netflix show where he helps people clean up their money messes in real time.

Other great resources:

- Get Good with Money by Tiffany Aliche

- The Total Money Makeover by Dave Ramsey

- Free podcasts and YouTube videos (literally search personal finance for beginners/single moms)

And let me just say this — the library is your friend. Don't want to spend money on books? Borrow them. For the FREE!

Practical Tools & Systems

- Budgeting Apps: YNAB (You Need a Budget), Every Dollar, or even a good old pen and notebook if you're like me. Sit down with your money at least twice a month.

- High-Yield Savings: Use online banks like Ally, SoFi, or Capital One to earn more interest on your savings. We want our money to make money while it sits.

- Savings Buckets: Save for Christmas, birthdays, back-to-school, or anything else with specific buckets inside your savings account. This way, they are not big expensive hits when they come.

You know they're coming, and you've planned for them.

- Automatic Transfers: Pay yourself first. Have your job split your check and send a portion directly into savings. Personally, I think 10% is a great amount. You can adjust to live on the other 90%, but if that feels just too tight right now, start with 1% or a set dollar amount like $20 a paycheck.

It's not about how much you save. It's about making it a habit.

My Journey: From Nothing to Stability

I'll never forget the day I moved out of my mom's house. I had been working again. I was budgeting, saving, doing the best I could with what I had. And we got approved for an income-restricted townhome.

I remember picking up the keys. Walking through the door. And crying.

No One Is Coming

We had nothing. No beds. No couches. No dishes. Just a home. My very first home. Mine.

We made a pallet on the floor that first night. And over time, we built. We got beds. A dining table. A couch. A TV. And every bit of it — I did on my own.

I had never lived alone before. I had always lived with family, roommates, or my ex. But now it was just me and my son, and I was doing it. And as scary as it was — it felt so damn good. Because I knew that everything I was doing, I was building with intention. With love. With resilience.

And that's what I want you to know too:

You can rebuild your life from nothing.

You can go from broke and broken to stable and thriving. I'm not special. I'm just committed. And so are you. Or else you wouldn't be here.

Apply the knowledge. Stay consistent. Don't try to be perfect — just try to be intentional.

Rebuilding from Nothing

You don't have to have it all figured out right now. You just need to take the next step.

Once you've created some stability, the next level is about elevation. It's time to shift from just staying afloat to building something solid — something that gives you options, freedom, and peace. The goal isn't just to survive paycheck to paycheck — it's to reach real financial security.

Budgeting is the foundation. Saving is necessary. But sis — let's be honest. We didn't come this far just to have "enough." We want overflow. We want options. We want more.

Let's talk about how to start creating multiple income streams that fit your life, your skills, and your goals.

Chapter 6

Creating Multiple Income Streams

In today's economy, having only one source of income is way too close to having none at all. Depending on one paycheck is like walking a tightrope without a safety net. One layoff, one budget cut, one unexpected curveball, and suddenly you're scrambling. As a single mom, you cannot afford that kind of vulnerability. Your children are depending on you, and so are you. That's why creating multiple streams of income isn't just a good idea — it's essential.

Creating Multiple Income Streams

Let's be clear: I'm not saying you need to work three jobs or never sleep. I know you already have more on your plate than most. What I am saying is that you already have marketable skills, talents, experiences, and stories that can be turned into extra income. You just have to identify them and get creative.

And lucky for us — we're living in the age of technology, automation, and AI. Tools like ChatGPT make it easier than ever to brainstorm, create, and even execute on ideas. Here's a prompt to use right now (you're welcome):

"ChatGPT, given my experience in [insert experience], my talent in [insert talent], and my skills in [insert skills], what are 10 profitable side hustle ideas I can start with minimal investment? Break down simple steps for each."

I've used this prompt myself and the results were game-changing. Some ideas I had already thought of. Others were completely new. The point is — help is out there. Free help. You just have to use it.

Why You Need More Than One Stream

Multiple income streams = more options, more peace, and more power.

It's not just about luxury, sis. It's about stability. When you're not constantly checking your bank balance before filling up your gas tank, your energy shifts. When you can afford to treat your child to a random ice cream run or say yes to a weekend trip, that's the kind of freedom we're aiming for.

Budgeting is great. Saving is necessary. But let's be real — we want more than just surviving. We want breathing room. Overflow. Abundance.

And that comes from building income that doesn't rely solely on your 9 to 5.

Types of Income to Consider

1. Digital Products

Digital products are a powerful way to build income that becomes semi-passive over time. Yes, there's work on the front end, but once it's created, it can sell again and again.

Ideas for digital products:

- Printable planners or journals

- E-books or guides (on literally anything you know well)

- Templates or checklists

- Digital courses

Don't tell yourself you have nothing to offer. If you're a mom, you already know things people are googling every day. From potty training tips to meal planning hacks — your life experiences can help someone else.

2. Affiliate Marketing

You're already recommending products to your friends — might as well get paid for it. Affiliate marketing means you earn a commission when someone buys through your unique link.

Start with programs like:

- Amazon Associates

- TikTok Shop

- ShareASale

- LTK

Think about the things you use and love. That stroller that saved your back? The skincare routine that got you glowing? Talk about it. Share it. Get paid.

3. Content Creation

TikTok, YouTube, Instagram — platforms that pay creators for views, engagement, and influence. Now, don't panic. You don't need a million followers. There are people making hundreds (and thousands) from very small audiences.

You can:

- Join the TikTok Creator Rewards Program

- Monetize YouTube Shorts or videos

- Use social media to drive affiliate sales or promote your digital products

Just be authentic. Share your journey. Let people in. That's what builds trust — and trust leads to income.

4. Freelancing

Are you good at writing, editing, designing, customer service, social media management, video editing, admin work, or tutoring? Someone will pay you to do it.

Check out platforms like:

- Upwork

- Fiverr

- Freelancer

Start with your existing skill set. Think about what people at work ask you for help with. That's probably your zone of genius.

5. Service-Based Side Hustles

This was my first income stream outside of my job. I started braiding hair. I had learned to braid when I was 12 and had been doing it ever since. So, I took pictures, posted on Facebook Marketplace and Craigslist, and started taking clients.

It was time-consuming and required energy — but it helped pay the bills. And that's what mattered.

You might:

- Babysit

- Do hair or nails

- Offer cleaning services

- Become a virtual assistant

If it's a skill that helps someone else solve a problem — it can be monetized.

Practical Steps to Build Your Income

1. Brainstorm Your Options
Use ChatGPT, journal, or whiteboard your skills, experiences, and interests. Think about what you're good at and what people often come to you for help with.

2. Choose One to Start
Don't try to do all the things at once. Pick the one that feels the most doable. The most exciting. The most aligned with your current life.

3. Make a Plan

- What's the first step?

- What tools or platforms do you need?

- How will you market it?

- How much time can you realistically dedicate each week?

4. Leverage Free Tools

- Use ChatGPT to plan content, create outlines, or write product descriptions.

- Use Canva for design.

- Use social media to promote.

5. Start Small, Stay Consistent

You don't need a perfect launch. You need action. Imperfect, messy, learning-as-you-go action.

My Journey: From Braiding to Building

I started with braiding. And now I've done affiliate marketing. I've created content that not only resonates but also earns. I've made money from knowledge I used to think was just "my story."

The confidence that comes from knowing you can generate income outside of your job is unmatched.

You stop feeling stuck. You stop feeling scared. You start feeling empowered.

You realize you don't need permission. You don't need someone to save you. You are the safety net. You are the source.

And when the money starts flowing in from different directions– It's like a light switch flips. You're no longer panicking about bills — you're planning for vacations. You're stacking for your emergency fund. You're investing in your dreams.

Multiple income streams = financial security and peace of mind.

Here's What You Need to Remember

Please don't sit in self-doubt and tell yourself you don't have anything to offer. You do. You've got experience, wisdom, and grit. That's the secret sauce.

No One Is Coming

If someone is paying you to do something already, you have a skill. If you've gone through something and come out stronger — you have a story. If you've learned how to make life easier, smoother, or more joyful in some area — you have value.

You can turn that into income. You can build financial security. You can stop living in survival mode and step into overflow.

You just have to start.

And once you do, and those extra dollars start coming in, it's time to talk about what to do with that money. Because we're not just going to earn — we're going to grow, multiply, and build generational wealth.

Chapter 7

Mindset Shifts for Wealth Building

If you grew up anything like me, then you probably heard phrases like, "Money doesn't grow on trees?" or "We have food at home."

I remember growing up, my mom was a single mom raising four girls, and money was tight. One of the ways my mom kept costs down was by strictly regulating how much water we used. We had five-minute showers, and they were timed. I'll never forget being in the shower, completely lathered up, when suddenly—BANG BANG BANG!

"Uh-uh! Your time is up! Hurry up, wash it off, and get out—you're not running up my water bill!"

It's crazy I can still hear my mom's voice now!

Those moments stuck with me. And I wasn't the only one—when my sisters and I finally moved out on our own, the very first thing we all did was take a long, hot shower. It was a small thing, but it was a symbolic of something bigger: how we had been conditioned to think about money in terms of lack, restriction, and survival.

If you grew up hearing "money doesn't grow on trees" or "we can't afford that," chances are you developed a scarcity mindset around money. And that mindset is keeping you broke. Studies show that people who believe wealth is out of their reach tend to make financial decisions that keep them in survival mode— paying the minimum on bills, avoiding investing, or never thinking long-term.

Morgan Housel, author of The Psychology of Money, said it best: "Your personal experiences with money make up maybe 0.0000001% of what's happened in the world, but maybe 80% of how you think the world works." Meaning, if you've only ever seen financial struggle, it's easy to believe that's all that's possible. But it's not.

This is where we start shifting that belief system. Because the truth is, financial security is available to you—but you have to believe it's possible first.

The Psychology of Wealth & Abundance

If you've ever scrolled through social media and ended up on the business, entrepreneurship, or wealth-building side of the algorithm, you might have come across James Dumoulin and the School of Hard Knocks. His platform is dedicated to interviewing some of the world's wealthiest people—millionaires, billionaires, industry leaders—and asking them questions about money: How old were you when you made your first million? What did you do to become wealthy? What advice do you have for others trying to achieve the same success?

One of his go-to questions is, "Have you been broke before?" And the answer, more often than not, is a resounding YES. Some of these highly successful people have even lost everything and had to build it back from scratch. (Sounds familiar, doesn't it?) These aren't just the privileged elite who had it handed to them—these are people from all backgrounds who figured out how to create wealth, not because of where they started, but because of how they think.

This is the key takeaway—it's not about where you start. It's not about how much money you have right now, what kind of job you're working, or even the skills you currently have. It's about the psychology of wealth. The difference between struggling financially and thriving comes down to one very important thing: How you think about money.

Wealthy people don't just have more money— they think differently about money. Instead of focusing on what they don't have, they focus on how to create more. They see money as a tool, not a burden. They don't let fear keep them from investing, starting businesses, or taking calculated risks. They understand that money flows, that setbacks are temporary, and that opportunities exist everywhere if you know how to look for them.

So, let the shift start here. Instead of saying, "I can't afford this," start asking, "How can I afford this?" Instead of thinking, "I'll never have money like that," start asking, "What do I need to learn to get there?"

I want to be very clear—I'm not talking about reckless spending or pretending money doesn't matter. It's about training your brain to find solutions instead of stopping at obstacles. The way you think about money shapes the way you act with money. And those actions are what ultimately build financial freedom.

And the good news is you can start changing your money mindset right now. And once you do, you'll see your financial situation start shifting too.

Breaking the Cycle of Financial Struggle for Your Kids

My mom was my primary parent, the one handling the day-to-day responsibilities, and I saw firsthand how she managed our household finances. She would sit in bed with random sheets of paper, scribbling numbers, crossing things out, and trying to make it all work. My dad, who I spent weekends with, had a different approach—he was always the one reminding me that some things were just too expensive or unnecessary, like the shoes I wanted or the Pokémon cards I begged for.

They both always made do. My childhood was amazing, full of love, laughter, and the simple joys of life. I never thought of us as broke or poor—because we weren't. We weren't severely impoverished or struggling to survive, but we also weren't rolling in the dough either. We were a simple, middle-class family. We had what we needed, but money never felt easy.

It was never talked about in an abundant way. It wasn't something that flowed freely or was seen as an opportunity. Instead, it was something to be careful with, something that always needed to be stretched, and could easily become a problem. The adults in my life never seemed to have much of it—just enough to survive, to keep things running, to live a simple life. But it was always a stressor.

The truth is, that kind of mindset gets passed down—whether we realize it or not.

By the time I became an adult, I found myself repeating the same financial patterns I had grown up watching. I wasn't making intentional financial decisions—I was just surviving. Living paycheck to paycheck, juggling bills, and constantly feeling like money was something that controlled me instead of something I controlled.

And one day it hit me: if I didn't change the way I handled money, my child would grow up seeing the same cycle play out.

Here's something that might surprise you: Children form their core money beliefs by age 7—long before they ever have their own bank account or paycheck. (Cambridge University, 2013). That means by the time they're old enough to earn money, their attitudes, fears, and behaviors around money are already shaped—not by what we teach them directly, but by what they see.

Your kids are watching.

They notice how you talk about money. They hear it when you say, "We can't afford that," or when you stress about bills. They see if you avoid looking at your bank account or hesitate to spend even on things that matter. They pick up on your financial stress, even if you don't think they do.

But just as they can absorb financial struggle, they can also absorb financial empowerment.

If they see you building an emergency fund, improving your credit, setting financial goals, and making intentional money moves, they start to see money as something they can control. Instead of learning that money is stressful and scarce, they learn that money is a tool—something that can be managed, grown, and used to create security and opportunity.

This is where the cycle ends.

You're not just changing your financial future—you're changing theirs too. You're giving your children a new blueprint, one that's built on intention, security, and possibility. You're breaking generational cycles, one choice at a time.

And now that you've laid the foundation—emotionally, financially, and mentally—it's time to build something even greater.

It's time to reinvent yourself.

Part 3

Reinventing Yourself

Chapter 8

Designing the Life You Truly Want

There's something powerful that happens when you hit rock bottom and have to start over—you get to rebuild from scratch. I know it doesn't always feel like a blessing in the moment. In fact, it probably feels more like loss, heartbreak, and a thousand unanswered questions. But underneath all that rubble is something beautiful: a clean slate.

You have a chance right now to decide what this next chapter of your life looks like. Not based on your past. Not based on what your ex wanted. Not based on what your parents expected. This time, you get to choose for you.

The dream you once had for your life might've included someone who's no longer here. The future you pictured might've died when that relationship ended. And that hurts. But the beautiful flip side of that is now you're free to dream a new dream—one that's yours and yours alone.

So, I want you to take some time. Grab a journal, open your notes app, pull out a blank Google Doc— whatever works for you—and I want you to daydream. Daydream wildly, unapologetically, like the entire universe is listening and ready to deliver.

What does your ideal life look like now? What kind of career do you want? What kind of money do you want to earn? What kind of home do you want to live in? What kind of woman do you want to be? Who do you want your kids to see when they look at you?

Don't hold back. Don't edit. Let yourself dream without limits—even if it feels unrealistic. Even if it feels so far away that it almost makes you laugh. Because sis, that's exactly where we want to start.

Finding Your Passion & Purpose

Let's talk about identity for a minute. Because if you're anything like me, motherhood and relationships consumed you. You became so focused on taking care of your household, your child, and your man, that you forgot who you were.

That's not shade. That's the truth for so many of us.

We shift into survival mode, into mom mode, into "make-it-work" mode. And somewhere in the middle of daycare pickups, school projects, basketball practices, and birthday party planning—we lose ourselves.

We stop doing the things that made us feel alive. We stop exploring. We stop dreaming. We stop asking, "What do I love to do just for me?"

And now it's the time to find her again.

Maybe you don't even know what you enjoy anymore—and that's okay. That was me too. I remember my therapist asking me, "What do you do for fun?" and I genuinely had no idea how to answer. I had to go back to square one and figure out who I was outside of being a mom and someone's partner.

I've always loved books. As a kid, I could get lost in a good story for hours, and that love for reading never went away. So, when I started rediscovering myself, I leaned into that love and started a book club. Not just an online one—I mean a real, in-person women's book club.

As an extrovert, I need connection. I thrive in community. Being around other women, talking about powerful stories, sharing laughs, tears, and aha moments over good books—it filled my cup in a way I didn't even realize I needed. Starting that book club helped me rebuild parts of myself that had been quiet for too long. It gave me something to look forward to and reminded me that joy can be found in the simplest things: a good book and good company.

You won't know what you enjoy until you give yourself permission to explore. Try new hobbies. Join a local meetup. Go to events solo. Revisit things you used to love or dabble in things you've never tried. This part should be fun. Think of it as dating yourself.

You're not "just a mom." You're a whole, complex, beautiful woman. You deserve to feel fulfilled outside of your motherhood. Your kids benefit when you're happy, energized, and living with purpose.

Creating Your Ideal Life Blueprint

Once you've allowed yourself to dream—and I mean really dream—it's time to create the blueprint.

This is where we shift from vision to execution. From daydreaming to doing. You don't just want a cute life on paper—you want to actually live it. And that means creating goals that you can move toward.

Start by looking at the life you just envisioned. That dream life. That future you love.

Now ask yourself:

- What steps do I need to take to get there?

- What do I need to learn?

- What habits do I need to form?

- What people, places, or patterns do I need to release?

You don't have to do it all at once. You won't. And that's okay. The most powerful changes happen one step at a time.

There's a quote I love: "How do you eat an elephant? One bite at a time."

That's how we're going to approach this glow-up. One decision at a time. One habit at a time. One small goal after the next.

When I set a goal to become a homeowner, it felt impossible at first. I was broke, living at my mom's house, with bad credit and no savings. But I started where I was. I worked on my credit. I started saving small. I researched loan programs. I chipped away at that dream, step by step, until one day, I had keys in my hand and tears in my eyes. That was my glow-up moment.

And trust me—your moment is coming too.

SMART Goals: Your Step-by-Step System

Let's make it practical.

I want you to break your dream down into SMART goals:

- S = Specific

- M = Measurable

- A = Attainable

- R = Relevant

- T = Time-bound

Don't just say, "I want to be rich." Be specific: "I want to earn $5,000 a month in passive income."

Don't just say, "I want to lose weight." Say: "I want to lose 20 pounds by December."

Make it measurable so you can track progress. Make it attainable so it feels realistic. Make it relevant to the life you're designing. And put a date on it. Because goals without deadlines turn into wishes.

There's this book I love called The 12-Week Year. It teaches you how to compress your goals into 12-week sprints instead of giving yourself a whole year. That sense of urgency is what gets results. That's how businesses move. And that's how we're moving from now on.

Your glow-up deserves structure.

Progress Over Perfection

Let me say this loud and clear: you don't have to do it perfectly.

You will have setbacks. You will have days where you feel overwhelmed. Days where you don't stick to the plan. Days where life just life's. That doesn't mean you've failed.

Progress is not linear. It's messy, it's real, and it's human. But as long as you're still moving, you're still winning.

You're allowed to pivot. You're allowed to course-correct. You're allowed to start again as many times as you need to.

The goal is to keep showing up. Keep moving forward. Keep building that life you deserve.

Your Life, Your Rules

This is your chance to rewrite the rules.

You don't need to fit into anyone else's box. You don't need to live by your ex's expectations. You don't need to follow society's tired script about what a single mom's life should look like.

You get to decide what success looks like for you. You get to define what happiness means to you.

Maybe your dream life is a six-figure career and a luxury high-rise condo. Maybe it's a quiet home in the suburbs with a garden and a book club. Maybe it's traveling the world with your kids, living free and unbothered.

Whatever it is—claim it. Own it. Build it.

Here's What You Need to Remember

- You are not too broken to rebuild.

- You are not too late to start over.

- You are not too lost to find your way.

You are in the process of becoming everything you've ever wanted. And it starts now.

Designing the Life You Truly Want

You're not just healing—you're rising. You're not just surviving—you're creating. You're not just dreaming—you're designing.

This is your comeback season.

And now that you've started designing the life you truly want, it's time to become the woman who lives it.

Chapter 9

Becoming Her

As you continue to transform yourself—and in turn, transform your life—you'll notice something start to happen. You begin to shed the layers of who you used to be. The old beliefs, the outdated patterns, the watered-down version of you that was playing small or living for someone else. You're stepping into your next best version. You're becoming her.

But let's be clear: her isn't some trendy aesthetic or social media version of perfection. She's who you decide she is. She's the woman you've envisioned during this glow-up. She's the version of you who owns her power, protects her peace, and walks boldly in her truth.

And because you've worked this hard to become her, you have to protect her.

People will try to pull you back into who you used to be—especially people who were comfortable with that version of you. Friends, family, even your ex might try to hold you to your past. But you're not her anymore. You're growing. You're glowing. And you've got places to go.

This chapter is about staying in your power. About developing the emotional resilience and mental toughness it takes to not just reach the next level—but to maintain it.

Protecting Your Peace in the Face of Growth

When you start leveling up, people notice. Some will cheer you on. Some will question it. And some will try to pull you back down.

That's why you have to protect this version of you like your life depends on it. Because in a way—it does.

There's a concept Mel Robbins teaches called the "Let Them" theory. It's all about letting people be who they are, do what they do, and think what they think—without it disrupting your peace.

Let them judge you. Let them doubt you. Let them gossip. Let them go.

Your job isn't to control what others do. Your job is to protect your energy and stay focused on your growth. When you stop reacting to everything and start choosing your peace instead, you step into a whole new level of personal power.

Another game-changer for me was The Four Agreements. The second agreement of the four is: Don't take anything personally. And whew—if you can master that, you're unstoppable.

Because sis, not everything is about you. People's opinions, projections, shade, or silence are more about them than they are about you. And when you stop taking it on, you stay free. Free to keep growing. Free to keep becoming. Free to protect the peace you've worked so hard for.

Transforming Pain into Power & Prosperity

I know you've been through some things. I know the pain of heartbreak, betrayal, abandonment, and starting over has left some scars. But let me remind you of something: you're still here.

That means your story didn't end in the pain. It's evolving into power.

You don't have to pretend the past didn't happen. You just have to stop letting it define you. Let it refine you instead. Every hardship you've survived has taught you something valuable. Every tear has watered the soil of your next season.

Your pain has purpose.

When you learn the lessons, you break the cycles. You gain wisdom. You grow emotional muscle. You raise your standards. You move differently.

And not only do you grow—you get to pass that wisdom on. To your children. To your future self. To the next woman who will need the light you're carrying.

This is how you take your power back. This is how you turn wounds into wisdom. This is how you rise.

Self-Care Isn't Optional—It's Required

Now, let's talk about something we all tend to put last on the list: self-care.

I know you're busy. You've got work. You've got kids. You've got bills. You're out here being everything to everyone.

But sis, let me tell you—you can't pour from an empty cup.

Becoming Her

Self-care is not a luxury. It's not something you get to when everything else is done. It's the foundation for everything you're building.

You can't glow-up if you're burnt out.

And no, self-care doesn't have to mean spa days and shopping sprees. It can be simple. Accessible. Free.

- Taking a walk and getting fresh air.

- Listening to music that lifts your spirit.

- Journaling your thoughts, emotions, and wins.

- Reading a few pages of a book.

- Saying "no" without guilt.

- Taking a nap.

- Drinking more water.

- Creating a calming bedtime routine.

No One Is Coming

One of the best things I ever did for myself was create a solid morning routine. I started waking up at 4:30 a.m. so I could have time for me before the demands of the day took over.

And no, I don't jump right out of bed. I give myself a few moments to breathe, stretch, and ease into the day. Then I follow a version of the 5 a.m. Club routine:

- First 20 minutes: Move your body. I jump rope, walk, or do a quick YouTube workout. It gets my blood flowing, wakes me up, and releases endorphins.

- Second 20 minutes: Reflect. I journal, do a devotional, or write down what I'm grateful for and what I'm excited about.

- Third 20 minutes: Grow. I read a personal development book, watch a YouTube video, or learn something new—like trading options, which I got into a while ago.

That first hour of the day is mine. And it makes all the difference. I show up better at work, with my kids, in my mindset, in my confidence. It grounds me. It energizes me. It reminds me that I matter too.

Self-care is about energy management. If you want to become her, you need to protect your energy like it's your most valuable currency—because it is.

Your Inner World Creates Your Outer World

Everything you're building—this new identity, this new life—starts from within. You're becoming a woman who thinks differently, believes differently, acts differently.

And over time, your outer life will reflect that.

This is your glow-up. This is your elevation. You are no longer settling, shrinking, or sacrificing your peace. You are walking in your purpose. You are honoring your evolution.

You are becoming her.

Let this chapter be your reminder that this process is sacred. Protect it. Nurture it. Be proud of how far you've already come. Because the best isn't behind you—it's ahead of you. And you're walking toward it with clarity, confidence, and a renewed sense of self.

You didn't just survive. You rose. You didn't just rebuild—you became brand new. You've stepped into this higher version of yourself, and now it's time to live like her—boldly, unapologetically, and fully.

Chapter 10

Living Your New Life Fully

You didn't come this far just to come this far. All the tears, the late nights, the deep self-reflection, the fights with your inner critic, the sacrifices—you didn't do all that for nothing. You've worked to heal emotionally. You've rebuilt financially. You've begun to rediscover your passions, reconnected with your purpose, and most importantly, you've remembered who the hell you are.

This chapter is about living in that truth. Not half-heartedly. Not conditionally. Fully.

You deserve to live a life that feels good—not just one that looks good on the outside. It's time to enjoy the woman you've become and embrace the life you're creating with confidence, intention, and joy.

Living Boldly and Unapologetically

You've been through enough. The last thing you need to do now is dim your light to make other people comfortable. This version of you? The one who healed, leveled up, and learned how to carry herself with grace and grit? She deserves to shine.

Living your life fully means allowing yourself to feel joy again. It means laughing without guilt. Saying yes to fun. Saying no to anything that drains you. It means making memories with your kids, treating yourself to the things you once talked yourself out of, and creating new experiences that light your soul on fire.

It means deciding that you're no longer going to be a background character in your own story.

This is your life. You are the main character now. Own it.

Inspiring Others

One of the most powerful things about healing and evolving is that it creates a ripple effect. Whether you realize it or not, your journey is going to impact other people—especially other women.

There are women right now, where you were not that long ago— heartbroken, overwhelmed, scared, and unsure how they're going to make it through. Just like you once were.

And they need to know what you now know: that it gets better.

That's the reason I wrote this book. Because I remember being in the thick of it, scrolling through social media or pacing around the house at night, desperately wishing there was someone who could tell me it was going to be okay. Not in a vague, fluffy way — but from someone who had actually been through it.

I couldn't find that book then. So, I wrote it now. For you.

And someday, when you're on the other side of your glow-up and a friend, a cousin, or even a stranger is going through their storm — you'll be able to look them in the eyes and say, "I've been there. And I got through it. So will you."

Leave your rope hanging behind you, sis. Someone else in the dark might need it.

Keep Growing — This Isn't the End

I wish I could tell you that this was the final boss. That after healing from heartbreak and reclaiming your life, everything would be smooth sailing.

But life will still life.

Living Your New Life Fully

You'll still face challenges. There will be moments when the pressure feels like too much or you find yourself questioning everything again. That's normal. This isn't about never having setbacks. It's about building the resilience to bounce back faster every time you do.

Growth is a lifelong journey. Healing is ongoing. And the good news is—you now have the tools to navigate whatever comes next.

You've already survived 100% of your worst days. You've proven to yourself that you can rise, rebuild, and reinvent your entire life.

So, when life throws a curveball—and it will—don't panic. Don't retreat. Just breathe. Ground yourself. And remember who the hell you are.

You're not just a single mom. You're a powerhouse.

You're not just surviving anymore. You're thriving.

A Reminder: You're Doing This for You—and Them

Let's not forget who else is watching: your kids. They're watching how you handle life. How you rise. How you cry, dust yourself off, and keep going.

They're learning what strength looks like. What self-respect sounds like. What healing and wholeness and self-love really mean.

Every time you choose peace over pettiness, growth over comfort, and love over fear—you're teaching them what's possible.

So, if you ever need motivation to keep going, just look at them. And then look in the mirror. You're doing it. For both of you.

Living in Your New Energy

You've done the work. You've cried the tears. You've read the books, listened to the podcasts, sat in silence with your own thoughts, and faced the hard truths.

Now it's time to live.

Live in your new energy. Live in your joy. Live in your confidence. Live in your healing.

Stop shrinking. Stop questioning whether you're ready. You are. You're already becoming everything you once prayed for.

So, walk in it.

If You Don't Remember Anything Else from This Chapter, Remember This:

You didn't survive all that just to go back to who you used to be.

Conclusion

If you made it here—truly made it to the end of this book—I just want to pause and say: I'm proud of you.

You didn't just read a book. You walked through a journey. You faced the truth. You stared heartbreak in the face. You gave yourself permission to cry, to process, to release. You took radical ownership of your life. And whether you feel it fully yet or not—you are no longer the same woman who started this journey.

You've evolved.

Conclusion

This book wasn't about giving you a magic fix. It wasn't about perfection or pretending the hard stuff doesn't exist. It was about walking you through the mess, the healing, the rebuilding, and the becoming. Page by page. Chapter by chapter. Step by step.

It was about helping you realize that no one is coming—but that's not the tragedy. That's the transformation.

Because when you realize that you are the one you've been waiting for... that's when the magic begins.

You Did the Work. Now Keep Doing It.

Healing isn't linear. You will still have moments where you doubt yourself. Where old wounds resurface. Where you wonder if you're really "over it" or just distracted. That's okay. That's human.

But now you have the tools. You have the mindset. You have the power.

You know how to protect your peace. You know how to get your money together. You know how to spot red flags from a mile away. You know how to hold boundaries, speak life over yourself, and create goals that actually stick. You know how to get back up every single time you fall.

And most importantly, you know who you are now.

So, keep showing up for her. Keep choosing her. Keep becoming her. Every single day.

Your Story Isn't Over—It's Just Getting Good

I know it might feel like this book is the end of something. But what if it's the beginning of everything?

What if this is the moment where your whole life shifts? Where you walk into rooms with your head held higher? Where you fall in love again—with yourself, with your purpose, maybe even with someone new (if you want to)? What if this is the version of you your younger self was dreaming of?

Conclusion

What if you are finally stepping into the life you were always meant to live?

Don't stop here. This isn't the end. This is your origin story. This is your new chapter. This is your power season.

And you don't owe anyone an explanation for how you got here. You just owe it to yourself to keep going.

A Final Word from Me to You

Writing this book healed a part of me too. It reminded me of how far I've come, how much I've grown, and how deeply I want other women—especially single moms—to know their strength. Their power. Their potential.

This book is a rope. And you grabbed it.

Now, if you feel led to, leave it hanging for someone else behind you.

No One Is Coming

Recommend it. Gift it. Repost your favorite quote. Share your story. Because when women rise together, everything changes.

And to every single mom reading this:

You are not broken. You are not behind. You are not alone. You are not done.

You are brilliant. You are capable. You are worthy. And you are already becoming everything you thought you lost.

You just forgot for a minute who the hell you were.

But now? Now you remember.

And when you remember—there's no stopping you.

See you at the top, sis.

With love,
Janaia

Conclusion

Resources & Suggested Reading

For Healing, Growth & Glow-Ups

These books have inspired me and supported my own journey—and I know they'll do the same for you. Some were mentioned in this book, others are bonus gems I've personally loved or believe you'll benefit from.

Healing & Personal Empowerment

- Let Them by Mel Robbins
  A powerful guide to letting go of control, reclaiming your peace, and mastering emotional resilience. If you're becoming her, this one's a must.

- The Four Agreements by Don Miguel Ruiz
  Short, deep, and transformational. The second agreement, don't take anything personally, will change how you move through the world.

- Year of Yes by Shonda Rhimes
  Say yes to yourself, your joy, your dreams. This book is funny, inspiring, and ridiculously relatable.

- You Are a Badass by Jen Sincero
  No fluff, all fire. This one helps you stop doubting and start thriving—with humor and straight talk.

Money, Abundance & Wealth Mindset

- The Psychology of Money by Morgan Housel
  Money isn't just about numbers—it's about behavior. This book helps you understand why you do what you do with money.

- I Will Teach You to Be Rich by Ramit Sethi
  A real-talk guide to money that's easy to understand, fun to read, and doesn't shame you for liking iced coffee or travel.

- Get Good with Money by Tiffany Aliche (The Budgetnista)

A 10-step system for financial wholeness,
especially empowering for women rebuilding
their financial lives.

- The Total Money Makeover by Dave Ramsey
  Old-school and straight to the point. If you need
  a solid debt payoff game plan, this one's for you.

- Rich Dad Poor Dad by Robert Kiyosaki
  A classic. Simple but eye-opening lessons on
  assets, wealth-building, and changing how we
  think about money.

Mindset & Habits

- Mindset: The New Psychology of Success by
  Carol S. Dweck
  Why your mindset matters more than you
  think—and how to shift from stuck to
  unstoppable.

- Atomic Habits by James Clear
  If you want practical steps to change your habits,

improve your life, and create consistency, start here.

- The 12-Week Year by Brian P. Moran
  Ditch New Year's resolutions and achieve your goals faster using this high-impact system.

Reinvention & Creating the Life You Want

- Boss Up! by Lindsay Teague Moreno
  Perfect for moms ready to build their own empire and stop playing small.

- Everything is Figureoutable by Marie Forleo
  A mantra and mindset to carry you through anything. Practical, encouraging, and fun.

- Big Magic by Elizabeth Gilbert
  Tap into your creativity, trust your intuition, and start living more boldly.

About the Author

Janaia Secrest-Holden is a writer, speaker, and real-life glow-up expert for single moms rebuilding from rock bottom. After healing from heartbreak, financial struggle, and starting over with nothing, she made it her mission to help other women do the same—without the fluff, the judgment, or the fake-it-'til-you-make-it energy.

Her voice is bold, relatable, and rooted in truth. She believes in owning your story, building your power, and creating a life that feels as good as it looks. Janaia is also the founder of The Single Mom Glow-Up Circle—a free, private Facebook community for women ready to rise.

If this book spoke to you, come join the tribe. Share your story and connect with other women who get it at www.facebook.com/groups/thesinglemomglowupcircle

www.ingramcontent.com/pod-product-compliance
Lightning Source LLC
Chambersburg PA
CBHW070342130626
46556CB00007B/2985